THE SONGS TELL THE STORY

BY JANET DENISON

Copyright © 2019 Christian Parenting

Reprinted 2022

All rights reserved.

This book or any portion thereof may not be reproduced or used in any manner whatsoever without the express written permission of the publisher except for the use of brief quotations in a book review.

Cover and interior illustrations: Adaptation from Adobe Stock. stock.adobe.com

Scripture quotations are from the ESV® Bible (The Holy Bible, English Standard Version®), copyright © 2001 by Crossway, a publishing ministry of Good News Publishers. Used by permission. All rights reserved.

Printed in the United States of America First Printing, 2019

17304 Preston Rd, Suite 1060 Dallas, TX 75252-5618

www.ChristianParenting.org

THE SONGS TELL THE STORY

BY JANET DENISON

christian parenting

A NOTE FOR PARENTS

Parents, your kids can read this devotional by themselves and glean much from it. However, they'll learn so much more if you take five to ten minutes and read it with them.

With twenty-five entries, if you start on December 1, you'll end this devotional on Christmas Day.

Once you've read a day together, discuss the main topic. See if your children know these songs, or the stories behind the songs, or the reason we sing these songs.

You may even want to queue up the music after reading so that their enjoyment (and yours) of these classic Christmas carols increases.

You may find yourself learning a thing or two as well.

And it's in that deeper knowledge of the stories of these songs that I pray you'll experience the kind of joy we sing about so often at Christmas, the joy that revels in Christ our King becoming Jesus a baby, "born that man no more may die."

P.S. My editor said I couldn't include lyrics to four songs because they don't belong to the public domain: Mary, Did You Know?, The Little Drummer Boy, Do You Hear What I Hear?, and Sweet Little Jesus Boy. However, this gives you the chance to play those songs for your kids and, of course, to sing them at the top of your lungs.

CONTENTS

The Song with an Incredible Answer 8

The Song My Dad Always Messed Up on Purpose 10

The Song that Makes Every Mom Cry 12

The Song of Joy Despite Sorrow 14

The Song of—Shh! 16

The Song that's Not a Christmas Song (Really) 18

The Song by Two Men Who Didn't Know Jesus 20

The Song that Makes Kids Think Some Angels are Named Harold 22

The Song You've Likely Known Forever 24

The Song about Being Born and Born Again 26

The Song about the King Whose Name We Can't Ever Pronounce Correctly 28

The Song that's Not about "Gold in Them Thar Hills" 30

The Song that Was Once about the Skulls of the Three Wise Men 32

The Song that's Secretly about Easter 34

The Song that You Could Have Sung Only in Latin 36

The Song that Took a Year to Get to 38

The Song Made Famous by a Famous Singing Family 40

The Song with the Wrong Number 42

The Song Inspired by Laughing Babies 44

The Song I Lose My Breath While Singing 46

The Song about the Boy We Sometimes Forget 48

The Song about Electrified Shepherds 50

The Song with a Tragic Origin Story 52

The Song about Light despite Dark Days 54

The Song that Gets to the Heart of Christmas 56

THE SONG WITH AN INCREDIBLE ANSWER

"What Child Is This?"

What Child is this who, laid to rest
On Mary's lap, is sleeping?
Whom angels greet with anthems sweet
While shepherds watch are keeping?

This, this is Christ the King,
Whom shepherds guard and angels sing, Haste,
haste, to bring Him laud,
The Babe, the Son of Mary!

"WHAT CHILD IS THIS?"

Almost no one in the world realized that Jesus was Christ the King that first Christmas.

People weren't expecting their Messiah would be a baby boy, born in a stable. But Mary knew her baby was special, and the angels told the shepherds he was too. Those shepherds who went to find Jesus became the first people to tell the world about him.

William Chatterton Dix was thinking about that when he wrote the hymn "What Child is This?" When William was a young man, he moved to Glasgow, Scotland, and worked in an insurance business. But his favorite thing to do was writing poetry.

> **His favorite thing to do was writing poetry.**

William became very ill and was forced to stay in bed for a long time. In the 1800s, there were a lot of illnesses that doctors didn't have the medicine to cure. During this time, Mr. Dix became very discouraged and began to question whether God was real. Eventually, William began to read a lot of Christian books. He spent a lot of time praying. Eventually, he recovered from his illness and became a man of great faith.

The man who loved to write poetry began to write hymns for the church. "What Child Is This?" is part of a longer poem called *The Manger Song*. William's poem was set to a famous tune of the day called "Greensleeves," and people have been singing his Christmas hymn since 1865.

A lot of people know this famous hymn and sing these words at Christmastime. But, like William, they have a lot of questions about God:

- Is he real?
- Does he love me?
- Was Jesus really the Son of God?

I hope this book will help you remember the great truth about Christmas and about Christ. It is the same truth that Mary and the shepherds knew about the baby born in a Bethlehem stable.

If your friends ask, "What child is this?" you can tell them. The baby sleeping in Mary's lap was Jesus, and he was Christ the King. You can "make haste to bring him laud" (laud means honor.)

The Babe, the Son of Mary, is our Lord and Savior.

THE SONG MY DAD ALWAYS MESSED UP ON PURPOSE

"The First Noel"

The First Noel, the Angels did say
Was to certain poor shepherds in fields as they lay
In fields where they lay keeping their sheep
On a cold winter's night that was so deep.

THE FIRST NOEL

When I was a kid, we had a Christmas decoration that consisted of four angels, each holding a red candle. The angels sat on letters that spelled out N-O-E-L. My dad would often rearrange those angels and wait until someone noticed they now spelled out L-E-O-N or E-L-N-O. Every time my family sang "The First Noel" in church, people wondered why we were grinning at each other.

"The First Noel" might be one of the oldest hymns we have. Some think the tune was written in the 1200s, but the Christmas words were added six hundred years later. The word *noel* comes from a Latin word that means "to be born," but *noel* later came to mean Christmas. "The First Noel" means "The First Christmas."

> **The First Noel means "The First Christmas."**

We know people have been celebrating the birth of Jesus since the year 300 AD. It's almost the year 2023. That means people have been celebrating Christ's birthday for something like seventeen hundred years!

When you sing this song, think about all the people who have sung these same words before you. Abraham Lincoln might have sung "The First Noel." Neil Armstrong, the first man to walk on the moon, sang this hymn. Your great-great-grandparents and their great-great-grandparents probably sang these same words.

Now, here is some Christmas trivia about "The First Noel." Some of the words should probably be changed. We celebrate Christmas in December, so the hymn says, "On a cold winter's night that was so deep." Truthfully, Jesus was probably born sometime in the spring. The reason we know that is because the shepherds were living in the fields at night watching their sheep (Luke 2:8). They didn't do that until spring.

But, that trivia doesn't change the truth about Christmas. The first Christmas was announced by angels who appeared to shepherds in a field. People have been "announcing" and celebrating the story of Christ's birth ever since.

When someone says "Happy holidays," you can say "Merry Christmas." When someone is excited about Santa, you can be excited about the Christmas story. When you sing "The First Noel," you sing about the first Christmas, and your voice is joined with millions of others throughout history. People have always wanted to announce the true meaning of Christmas.

"The First Noel, the angels did say."

What will you announce about Christmas this year?

3

THE SONG THAT MAKES EVERY MOM CRY

"Mary, Did You Know?"

"MARY, DID YOU KNOW?"

Holiday hymns and songs are an important part of the Christmas season.

I remember the first time I ever heard the Christmas song "Mary Did You Know?" A woman chose to sing that song during the worship service. When she finished, a lot of us were blotting tears from our eyes. The words of that song caused us to think about the Christmas story in a new way.

The words were written in 1984 by a man named Mark Lowry. He had been asked to write a Christmas play, so he sat down with pen and paper and began to imagine Mary holding her newborn baby. He thought about all the things the baby Jesus would do once he became a man. Eventually, the words became a poem and, eight years later, a song.

Every new mom holds her baby and wonders about the life her child will have when he or she is grown. Mary knew her baby was special because God was his only Father. Jesus is the only baby in all of history who didn't have an earthly father too. Mary knew she held a miracle in her arms, but I don't think she could have imagined all the miracles her baby would do when he grew to be a man.

> **Jesus is the only baby in all of history who didn't have an earthly father too.**

We know Jesus would one day walk on water. We know that Jesus was born to save anyone who would choose him as their Lord. That is how Jesus makes a person "new." Second Corinthians 5:17 says, "If anyone is in Christ, he is a new creation." Jesus wasn't just Mary's baby boy. He became her Lord and Savior as well.

Do you ever wonder about the life you will have in the future?

God never has to imagine the future because he already knows the future. God told the prophet Jeremiah, "I know the plans I have for you" (Jeremiah 29:11). God said his plan was for our good, to give us hope and a future.

God had a plan for his Son's life, and he has a plan for you. How can you know his plan?

- Pray.
- Learn God's word.
- And walk with the leadership and power of his Holy Spirit.

When Jesus is your Lord, his Holy Spirit lives in you. He is your helper, your teacher, your counselor, and the One who will guide you to know God's plan.

Did you know that the baby boy in Mary's arms would one day be with you?

Jesus is everyone's most important Christmas gift. You can be thankful for that gift today.

THE SONG OF JOY DESPITE SORROW

"Go Tell It On The Mountain"

Go tell it on the mountain
Over the hills and everywhere
Go tell it on the mountain
That Jesus Christ is born

When I was a seeker
I sought both night and day
I asked the Lord to help me
And he showed me the way

"GO TELL IT ON THE MOUNTAIN"

Have you ever sung this hymn at Christmastime?

Almost every year, one of the grade levels is assigned this famous African-American spiritual. It's hard to say when this song was written. It was originally sung by people who had been forced into slavery in our country. Very few of those people were given the chance to learn how to read and write, but they created and sang some of our favorite songs.

John Wesley Work, Jr. was the son of a church choir director. He grew up in Nashville and earned a master's degree in Latin. He taught Latin and Greek, but his first love was always music. He began to collect and record the spiritual music that had been created by the people who were forced to be slaves. "Go Tell It on the Mountain" is one of the songs Mr. Work learned and then recorded in his book.

The people who first sang "Go Tell It on the Mountain" shared the same Christmas message the shepherds had announced. They wanted to proclaim "that Jesus Christ is born!"

Many of those early slaves had very hard lives, and their songs reveal their sadness. This Christmas hymn was a hymn of hope to people who needed it and a reminder that Jesus was born to offer us his strength and his direction for our lives, even in our struggles.

For some people, Christmas can be a hard season. You probably know someone who is needing to feel joyful this Christmas. Families go through struggles, friendships can be broken, and school can be difficult sometimes.

But the message of Christmas doesn't always have to be about happy moments.

Joy is possible even when happiness isn't. The message of Christmas is found in the words of the shepherds and those early slaves. "Jesus Christ is born," and Jesus can show us the way to his quiet, comforting joy.

Who needs that message today?

Will you "go tell it" to them soon?

"

He taught Latin and Greek, but his first love was always music.

THE SONG OF—SHH!

"Silent Night"

Silent night, holy night
All is calm, all is bright
Round yon virgin, mother and child
Holy infant, so tender and mild
Sleep in heavenly peace, oh
Sleep, sleep in heavenly, heavenly peace

"SILENT NIGHT"

Joseph Mohr was a Catholic priest in Austria. He sang in the choir and spent most of his life serving the people of Salzburg. He chose to live a simple life and died in poverty because he gave away what he had to those who needed it.

In 1816 Mr. Mohr wrote a poem called "Stille Nacht" and never knew that his poem would make him famous throughout the world. "Stille Nacht" is German for "silent or still night."

> **'Stille Nach' is German for silent or still night.**

It was the Christmas of 1818 when Joseph Mohr was asked to write a new hymn for the Christmas mass. The organ was always central to the music of the church, but tradition says that the organ wouldn't work that day. So, Joseph Mohr used the words of his poem and a guitar to compose the carol we know as "Silent Night." Joseph's now-famous guitar is kept at the Silent Night Museum in Austria.

"Silent Night" is still considered one of the most popular Christmas carols of all time, and most churches include that song in their Christmas Eve services. Something about his words causes people to imagine that first Bethlehem evening.

It was a quiet night, made holy because the Son of God had entered the world. He was born of a virgin, a woman who had not conceived her baby in the usual way. God was the Father of Jesus. Everything about that "silent night" was miraculous. God chose to enter the world as a baby boy who slept peacefully in his mother's arms. It was a holy night, different from all others.

Christmas can be a busy, hectic, joyfully noisy season. We get busy with family, friends, and fun. It's so important to remember that our Christmas celebration is very different from the way it used to be.

People used to decorate their Christmas trees on Christmas Eve and take them down on New Year's Day. People used to celebrate with the family and friends who lived nearby because travel wasn't possible. We have added so much to our Christmas celebration that it might not be easy to remember how it was for Mary.

Maybe all of us should put down our phones, turn off our electronic devices, and take time this Christmas season to have a "Stille Nacht," a silent night, so that we can remember that holy night.

I think Mary—and Joseph Mohr—would approve.

THE SONG THAT'S NOT A CHRISTMAS SONG (REALLY)

"Joy To The World"

Joy to the world, the Lord is come;
Let earth receive her King!
Let every heart prepare him room
And heaven and nature sing!
And heaven and nature sing!
And heaven . . . and heaven . . .
and nature sing.

"JOY TO THE WORLD"

"Joy to the World" is on most people's lists of Christmas favorites. Did you know that it wasn't even written as a Christmas carol?

Isaac Watts wrote a book of poems based on the psalms. He wanted people to read those Old Testament passages with a New Testament point of view. Watts wanted people to think of Jesus as their King when they read Psalm 98:7–9, which says, "Let the sea resound, and everything in it, the world, and all who live in it. Let the rivers clap their hands, let the mountains sing together for joy; let them sing before the Lord, for he comes to judge the earth. He will judge the world in righteousness and the peoples with equity."

Compare those words to: "Joy to the world the Lord is come; Let earth receive her King! . . . And heaven and nature sing! And heaven and nature sing! "Joy to the World" was written one hundred years after Isaac Watts had written his book. It is an adaptation of Psalm 98 from Isaac Watts' book.

Jesus is the King of Christmas, and that is what we are supposed to remember when we sing "Joy to the World."

The last stanza of that hymn says:

He rules the world with truth and grace
And makes the nations prove
The glories of His righteousness
And wonders of His love
And wonders of His love
And wonders, wonders of His love.

Isaac Watts wanted people to understand that God rules the world with truth and grace, but it is our job to help others know the "wonders of His love."

People need joy. People need Jesus to be their King. Jesus told his disciples, "These things I have spoken to you, that my joy might be in you, and your joy may be full" (John 15:11). He wanted them to have his joy, the joy that comes from choosing God as your King.

Will you make Jesus your King and live with his joy?

That is how you give "joy to the world."

Did you know that it wasn't even written as a Christmas carol?

THE SONG BY TWO MEN WHO DIDN'T KNOW JESUS

"O Holy Night"

O holy night! The stars are brightly shining,
It is the night of our dear Savior's birth.
Long lay the world in sin and error pining,
Till He appear'd and the soul felt its worth.
A thrill of hope, the weary world rejoices,
For yonder breaks a new and glorious morn.

Fall on your knees! O hear the angel voices!
O night divine, O night when Christ was born;
O night divine, O night, O night Divine.

"O HOLY NIGHT"

In 1847, a man named Placide Cappeau was asked to write a poem for a Christmas service. He was a poet but admitted that he didn't attend church very often. Nevertheless, he said yes to the request. He was riding in a bumpy coach on a dusty road in France when he wrote the words to "O Holy Night."

Cappeau was reading the gospel of Luke that day for inspiration. He began to imagine what it must have been like for Mary and Joseph the night Jesus was born. His thoughts became his poem. Because he felt that his poem had been inspired by God, he decided it should become a hymn, so Cappeau asked a Jewish friend if he would compose music for his words.

Adolphe Charles Adams was a famous composer who didn't celebrate Christmas. He was Jewish and didn't believe the subject of the poem was God's holy Son. But he wrote beautiful music for his friend's poem, anyway.

> **Very few people realize it was written and composed by two men who knew very little about Jesus.**

"O Holy Night" has been sung in churches around the world for hundreds of years. Very few people realize it was written and composed by two men who knew very little about Jesus.

Do you ever feel like you don't know enough to share your beliefs about Jesus? Do you get quiet when Jesus is talked about at your school or at a party? Sometimes it seems like the subject of Jesus is really just for preachers or Bible teachers on Sunday.

Jesus allows himself to be known by everyone. He can be seen in the miracles of nature, in the lives of believers, and in the words of the Bible. But, Jesus can also inspire and use people who don't have a strong faith.

Jesus was talking to his disciples before they went out to share their faith with others. They were worried they wouldn't know what to say. Jesus told them, "Do not be anxious how you are to speak or what you are to say, for what you are to say will be given to you in that hour" (Matthew 10:19).

God still inspires people today with great words and thoughts. If your friends are talking about Christmas, or Christ, and you want to help them believe, ask God what you should say. Let God's Holy Spirit give you his words and speak.

God gave words to two unlikely men, and Christians have been singing "O Holy Night" for hundreds of years.

What will God help you say today?

THE SONG THAT MAKES KIDS THINK SOME ANGELS ARE NAMED HAROLD

"Hark! The Herald Angels Sing"

Hark! The herald angels sing,
"Glory to the new-born King;
Peace on earth and mercy mild,
God and sinners reconciled!"

Joyful, all ye nations, rise,
Join the triumph of the skies;
With th'angelic host proclaim,
"Christ is born in Bethlehem!"

Hark! The herald angels sing,
"Glory to the new-born King!"

"HARK! THE HERALD ANGELS SING"

"Hark! The Herald Angels Sing" has always been one of the most popular hymns for Christmas. Hardly anyone knows that the words we sing are not the words that were originally sung. The first line of the hymn used to be, "Hark! How all the welkin rings!"

George Whitefield was a powerful preacher, and he made several changes to ancient hymns when he created his hymnal called *Collection*.

He knew that *welkin* meant the heavens or angels, but most of the people in his church didn't. So, he rewrote the first line so people would understand the meaning of the hymn a little better.

Aren't you glad he did?

A lot of people come to church during the Christmas season who don't come very often the rest of the year. They like to think about the birth of Christ and sing the Christmas hymns. Chances are, if you look around the church on Sunday morning, you will spot someone you know who doesn't come very often.

> **The first line of the hymn used to be, "Hark! How all the welkin rings!**

The Christmas season is a great time to invite people to experience Jesus all year. We celebrate Jesus' birth, but the last stanza of "Hark! The Herald Angels Sing" says:

Hail! The heaven-born Prince of Peace!
Hail! The Son of Righteousness!
Light and life to all he brings,
Risen with healing in his wings

Mild he lays his glory by,
Born that man no more may die:
Born to raise the son of earth,
Born to give them second birth.

Hark! The herald angels sing,
"Glory to the new-born King!"

Jesus was born so that we could one day be raised again to eternal life. Christmas is about Easter too. Jesus came to give us "second birth."

Will you look around and help others know?

If so, you announce the same glory the "welkin" announced that first Christmas.

THE SONG YOU'VE LIKELY KNOWN FOREVER

"Away In A Manger"

Away in a manger,
No crib for a bed,
The little Lord Jesus
Lay down his sweet head.

The stars in the sky
Look down where he lay,
The little Lord Jesus,
Asleep on the hay.

"AWAY IN A MANGER"

This was probably one of the first Christmas hymns you ever learned. It was written with easy words and a simple melody so children would be able to sing it for Christmas.

No one knows who wrote the hymn, and the last stanza was added later, possibly written by or about Martin Luther. Reverend Luther was famous for his work to reform and strengthen the church during his day.

The church had begun to believe things the Bible didn't teach. Most people didn't own a Bible of their own, so they didn't know what to believe unless they were taught the truth by others.

Martin Luther worked hard to make certain the church was careful to teach God's word correctly.

The last stanza of "Away in a Manger" could have been Luther's thoughts and teaching. It says:

Be near me, Lord Jesus,
I ask Thee to stay
Close by me forever
And love me, I pray

Bless all the dear children
In Thy tender care
And take us to heaven
To live with Thee there.

> **No one knows who wrote the hymn.**

It's possible those words tell us what Martin Luther thought was most important about Christmas: Jesus came from heaven, to be born as a baby. Then he grew to be a man who gave his perfect, sinless life so that anyone who would believe in him could live in heaven.

But, the last words of "Away in a Manger" also remind us that Jesus is still with us. God gives every believer his Holy Spirit, who is the Person and Presence of Jesus today. Jesus is close to believers now and forever. We are in his "tender care" until he takes us to heaven to live with him there.

Martin Luther would have wanted believers to think about that truth at Christmas.

Will you think about it today?

THE SONG ABOUT BEING BORN AND BORN AGAIN

"Good Christian Men Rejoice"

Good Christian men, rejoice
With heart and soul and voice;
Give ye heed to what we say:
Jesus Christ is born today!
Ox and donkey before him bow,
and he is in the manger now.
Christ is born today!
Christ is born today!

"GOOD CHRISTIAN MEN REJOICE"

Some people date "Good Christian Men Rejoice" all the way back to the fourteenth century. During that period of history, there were a lot of people who were unable to read. Only the wealthy could afford an education. Almost no one had a Bible in their home, and there were no radios, newspapers, or televisions!

> **Almost no one had a Bible in their home, and there were no radios, newspapers, or televisions!**

Most of the time, preachers traveled from place to place to preach. Only the big cities had sermons or lessons each week. So, the churches found different ways for people to learn about God. They made stained glass windows that visually told a story from the Bible. They painted pictures that reminded people of biblical characters and stories. They taught people to sing hymns so they could learn and remember important truths from the Bible.

Whoever wrote "Good Christian Men Rejoice" wanted the people to sing about Christmas and rejoice. The author wanted people to know that Jesus was laid in a manger and that all of creation was supposed to "bow" before the baby who was also God's Son, a King. The author of the hymn wanted people to know that Christmas was about the fact that "Christ is born today."

Why *today*?

Every day, when someone becomes a Christian, they are "born again." Christ is "born" in their lives. The Bible says, "Therefore, if anyone is in Christ, he is a new creation. The old has passed away; behold, the new has come" (2 Corinthians 5:17).

How is someone born again?

Romans 10:9 answers that question: "If you confess with your mouth that Jesus is Lord and believe in your heart that God raised him from the dead, you will be saved."

I hope you and everyone in your family and circle of friends have been "born again." But, chances are, there is still someone you know who needs to choose to confess Jesus as Lord and believe that truth with their whole heart. If someone came to your mind when you read those words, pray for them.

Maybe this will be the first Christmas he or she will celebrate as a "born-again believer" with Christ as their Lord.

That would be a great reason for good Christians—and Christ—to *rejoice* today.

THE SONG ABOUT THE KING WHOSE NAME WE CAN'T EVER PRONOUNCE CORRECTLY

"Good King Wenceslas"

Good King Wenceslas looked out
On the Feast of Stephen
When the snow lay round about
Deep and crisp and even
Brightly shone the moon that night
Though the frost was cruel
When a poor man came in sight
Gath 'ring winter fuel

"GOOD KING WENCESLAS"

This hymn was inspired by the story of an ancient king who was made a saint after his death. He was known as Vaclav the Good, or King Wenceslaus.

It is actually kind of funny to listen to people sing this song. *Nobody* seems to know how to pronounce Wenceslaus or Wenceslas, as it is written in most of our hymnals.

> **There are actually more than thirty possible pronunciations, but the most common in English is *Wen – suh – sluhs*.**

The good news is, with more than thirty possibilities, you can't really go wrong. Just say it confidently and everyone will think you are right!

King *Whatever* had a really interesting story.

The people of the Czech Republic had fallen on hard times. Tradition says that King W was looking out his window and watched a poor man collecting wood. The king asked his servant to find out where the poor man lived and help him take meat, drink, and firewood to his home.

It was a very cold night, and the king's servant was struggling to walk in the snow. As the story goes, the king told his servant to step in his footprints. Miraculously, each time the servant placed his foot where the king's foot had been, his feet were warmed.

They delivered the food and helped the family. Soon, news of the king's generosity spread through the country, encouraging others to be generous too.

The last stanza of "Good King Wenceslas" says:

Therefore, Christian men, be sure
Wealth or rank possessing
Ye, who now will bless the poor
Shall yourselves find blessing.

Christmas is a time when we give to those we love and give to those in need. All of us can "bless the poor" with what we give, whether it be a lot or a little.

The amazing thing about giving is that, when we give what the Lord wants us to give, we find it to be a blessing in our lives as well.

Whom will you bless this Christmas?

May you be blessed for following the example of Good King You-Know-Who.

THE SONG THAT'S NOT ABOUT "GOLD IN THEM THAR HILLS"

"It Came Upon The Midnight Clear"

It came upon the midnight clear,
That glorious song of old,
From Angels playing near the earth,
To touch their harps of gold;

"Peace on the earth, good will to men,
From Heaven's all-gracious King."
The world in solemn stillness lay,
To hear the Angels sing.

"IT CAME UPON THE MIDNIGHT CLEAR"

This Christmas carol was written by an American pastor in 1849. Reverend Edmund Hamilton Sears only wrote two hymns in his life. One of them was "It Came Upon a Midnight Clear."

Reverend Sears lived in New England during a chaotic time in America's history. The Gold Rush had caused many men to leave their families behind and go to California because they were hoping to find gold and get rich.

History also records the mid-1800s as the time of the Industrial Revolution. Our country began to manufacture all kinds of materials in mass quantities using machines. These machines required skilled workers, and many families left their farms and moved to the big cities. The cities quickly became overcrowded as more factories were built.

American culture started to change as well. People didn't live with the same priorities of church and family that had once characterized the farming communities. Rather, they began to compete for jobs and gold. Those priorities caused Reverend Sears to grow concerned for American families and their faith and write these words of the hymn:

And ye, beneath life's crushing load,
Whose forms are bending low,
Who toil along the climbing way
With painful steps and slow;
Look now! for glad and golden hours
Come swiftly on the wing.
Oh rest beside the weary road,
And hear the angels sing!

American culture is still hectic, and many are competing for better jobs, more money, or greater popularity. Christmas can be an especially busy season of rushing around and spending money on what we hope will be perfect gifts.

Reverend Sears would suggest we sing his hymn and remember God's priorities at Christmas. Jesus was and is the only perfect Christmas gift. Let's "rest beside the weary road, and hear the angels sing."

What message did the angels sing?

"Peace on the earth, good will to men."

Those are God's Christmas priorities.

Will you make them yours?

THE SONG THAT WAS ONCE ABOUT THE SKULLS OF THE THREE WISE MEN

"I Saw Three Ships"

I saw three ships come sailing in,
On Christmas Day, on Christmas Day.
I saw three ships come sailing in,
On Christmas Day in the morning

"I SAW THREE SHIPS"

This is probably *not* a hymn you will sing in church this Christmas season. In fact, the lyrics of this hymn have been altered throughout the years, to change with the times.

> ...the era of castles, knights, and warring kings.

This hymn was written in the Middle Ages, the era of castles, knights, and warring kings. It was sung by wandering minstrels who traveled throughout the countryside, hoping to earn a living by singing songs like these.

Believe it or not, this song was originally written about a legend that some people believed was true. This legend taught that long ago, there were three ships that sailed to the Cologne Cathedral in Germany. Each ship carried a skull of one of the three wise men. (Now you know why the lyrics of this Christmas carol have changed over the years!)

Later, the lyrics were about different Bible characters who rode the ships to Bethlehem. Now, the words are about Mary and Joseph's journey to Bethlehem. We know that Mary and Joseph didn't take ships to Bethlehem, so the lyrics are simply written to remind us of their journey.

This hymn has many stanzas but one central theme: Christmas is about rejoicing over the arrival of Jesus.

In the Middle Ages, families would stand at the harbor and watch ships sail away, often with friends and family members they loved. There were no telegraphs, phones, or email. Ships often sank in high winds and storms. Sometimes, pirates or enemy vessels attacked these ships. When loved ones sailed away, remaining family and friends didn't know if they would ever see or speak to them again.

So, imagine their joy when seeing a returning ship, months or even years later. They would watch the ship get closer and closer, hoping the person they loved was arriving back home.

That is why "I Saw Three Ships" remains a Christmas carol today.

Christmas is a time to remember that Jesus, our Messiah, *arrived* in Bethlehem. But it is also a time to be reminded that, one day, Jesus will return.

Jesus told his disciples, "Let not your hearts be troubled. Believe in God; believe also in me. In my Father's house are many rooms. If it were not so, would I have told you that I go to prepare a place for you? And if I go and prepare a place for you, I will come again and will take you to myself, that where I am you may be also" (John 14:1–3).

Just as people rejoiced when they saw those ancient ships pull into the harbor, we will rejoice one day when Jesus returns. This Christmas, let's rejoice over the arrival of Jesus in Bethlehem and, one day, our arrival in heaven.

THE SONG THAT'S SECRETLY ABOUT EASTER

"Love Came Down at Christmas"

Love came down at Christmas,
Love all lovely, Love Divine,
Love was born at Christmas,
Star and Angels gave the sign

"LOVE CAME DOWN AT CHRISTMAS"

Christina Rossetti lived in London, England, when she wrote the words of the Christmas poem that eventually became the carol "Love Came Down at Christmas." Her entire family was students of literature, music, and art. Her brother, Dante Rossetti, was famous for his paintings.

Christina was inspired by the verses of 1 John 4 when she wrote her poem. That passage of Scripture is about the greatness of God's love and the calling God has given his people to love others as God loves them. First John 4:7–8 says, "Beloved, let us love one another, for love is from God, and whoever loves has been born of God and knows God. Anyone who does not love does not know God, because God is love."

Christina wanted people to remember that Christmas was the time God showed his great love to all of mankind. We could consider John 3:16 a Christmas verse: "For God so loved the world, that he gave his only Son, that whoever believes in him should not perish but have eternal life."

God loves every person in this world and wants everyone to be with him in heaven. But everyone makes wrong choices. The Bible calls our wrong choices "sin." God knew that, no matter how much we'd try to obey his word, we would never obey perfectly.

Only one person ever lived a "sinless" life. He was named Jesus by Mary and Joseph. He was born in Bethlehem and grew and "increased in wisdom and in stature and in favor with God and man" (Luke 2:52). Jesus taught his disciples and others and performed miracles.

Then, one day, Jesus died on a cross and was buried. Many people, even his disciples, thought they would never see him again. But Jesus rose from his grave, proving he had power over death.

We celebrate Christmas because of Easter. God loved us so much, he gave us his Son. One day, his Son will give people who believe in him eternal life in heaven.

What do we have to believe in order to go to heaven?

- That Jesus was born at Christmas and died on the Easter cross.
- That Jesus never sinned, which means that his life, sacrificed for our mistakes, can atone (pay for) our wrong choices.
- That Jesus saves every person who trusts in him as their Lord and Savior.

Love indeed came down at Christmas. He was wrapped in swaddling clothes and laid in a manger. Later, Jesus was wrapped in burial clothes and laid in a tomb. But he rose from the grave. Now he is in heaven, waiting to wrap his loving arms around us.

Have you received the gift of his love, your salvation?

All you need to do is ask.

THE SONG THAT YOU COULD HAVE SUNG ONLY IN LATIN

"O Come, All Ye Faithful"

O come, all ye faithful,
Joyful and triumphant,
O come ye, O come ye, to Bethlehem;
Come and behold him,
Born the King of angels;
O come, let us adore him, Christ the Lord.

"O COME, ALL YE FAITHFUL"

This favorite Christmas carol is sung every Christmas. It was probably written by more than one person, and the lyrics have changed over the years. The words were first written and sung in Latin. Some people wanted to translate the stanzas into English, but others told them not to do that.

It seems strange to us today, but, during that period of history, there were Christians who didn't believe a hymn should ever be sung in English. They thought Latin was the only language for hymns.

"O Come, All Ye Faithful" is one of the hymns that was "smuggled off" to England and translated there. Over time, some of the words and ideas were changed during translation. Additional stanzas were added, and others were removed from the original version. Now, "O Come, All Ye Faithful" is a selection of stanzas from more than one of those translated versions.

But the message of this great Christmas carol is still the same today. The people who wrote this hymn wanted us to think about the people who came to see the newborn King. The authors wanted us to worship and adore Jesus as they did. This hymn is for the faithful and reminds us that we are supposed to *worship* Christ as our Lord.

People come to church for lots of reasons at Christmastime, and churches are glad to welcome them. All of us will sing this hymn, but we need to think about the words as we are singing them. Jesus would want us to experience the same joy that the shepherds, Mary, Joseph, and the magi felt as they beheld the infant King in the manger.

You can look around the church on Sunday and watch people sing. Some sing the words but don't look very thoughtful about what they are singing. Others sing with their hearts, thinking of the words and singing them to God. Some don't look like they are singing at all, but they might be praising God with their hearts.

Jesus would want us to adore him, just like Mary and the wise men adored the infant Jesus. Will you come to worship and be faithful? You can be faithful to pray, faithful to sing, and faithful to listen to God's word preached.

As you sing "O Come, All Ye Faithful," will you be joyful? Are you triumphant, knowing that Christ is your King?

There might have been several authors of this Christmas carol, but they all hoped for the same thing as they wrote. They wanted to call all of the faithful to remember the manger scene in Bethlehem and joyfully worship Christ the Lord.

Will you sing this Christmas carol, *faithfully*?

Jesus would love that!

THE SONG THAT TOOK A YEAR TO GET TO

"O Little Town of Bethlehem"

O little town of Bethlehem,
How still we see thee lie;
Above thy deep and dreamless sleep
The silent stars go by.
Yet in thy dark streets shineth
The everlasting light;
The hopes and fears of all the years
Are met in thee tonight

"O LITTLE TOWN OF BETHLEHEM"

"O Little Town of Bethlehem" was written for children to sing, but, later, adults wanted to sing the carol as well. The words and the tune might have been written for children to imagine Christmas night in Bethlehem, but adults need to think about those moments too.

Phillips Brooks wrote this Christmas carol in 1865 for the children of the church he pastored in Philadelphia, Pennsylvania. Mr. Brooks wrote this hymn after a trip he'd made to Bethlehem.

It took the pastor an entire year to travel by ship to Europe and then to the Holy Land by horseback. Back then, very few pastors ever visited the homeland of Jesus because it was so hard to get there.

> **It took the pastor an entire year to travel by ship...**

It is about six miles from Jerusalem to Bethlehem. Phillips Brooks and his traveling companions mounted their horses and began to ride. About two hours later, they saw a beautiful town built into the nearby mountain. The homes had beautiful gardens, and the men commented it was the most beautiful town they had seen in the area.

They continued to ride, hoping to arrive at the cave where people believed Jesus had been born. Next, they saw the fields where people believed the shepherds had seen the star and the angels. In fact, there were still shepherds in that field, watching their sheep that day.

Phillips Brooks left the Holy Land and returned home to Philadelphia. Later, as the Christmas season arrived, the pastor was thinking about everything he had seen that day, and he wrote "O Little Town of Bethlehem."

Today, Bethlehem is in the part of Israel considered Palestinian land. Most of the people who live in Bethlehem are Muslim and don't worship the baby who was born in their city. There are some Christians still living in the area, but their number is very few.

Mr. Brooks' words would be a good prayer to pray for the many people living in Bethlehem today who don't realize Jesus was born to be *their* Lord too.

Wouldn't it be amazing if, once more, the dark streets of Bethlehem were made to shine with an "everlasting light"?

What if Jesus could be born again in the lives of Bethlehem's neighbors? What if Jesus could be born again in the hearts of *our* neighbors?

When you sing "O Little Town of Bethlehem," think about the people who live there today. Sing the words as a prayer for them: "O come to us; abide with us; our Lord, Emmanuel."

THE SONG MADE FAMOUS BY A FAMOUS SINGING FAMILY

"The Little Drummer Boy"

"THE LITTLE DRUMMER BOY"

Have you ever seen the movie *The Sound of Music*?

It is the story of the Von Trapp family and their escape from Austria during World War II. The movie was filmed as a musical because the family had become famous as a singing group. The Trapp Family Singers recorded the carol "The Little Drummer Boy," and that is why the Christmas carol gained popularity in 1955.

"The Little Drummer Boy" was originally written in the Czech-Slavic language as a lullaby. Later, in 1928, it was translated to English in the *Oxford Book of Carols*. But it was a woman from Missouri named Katherine Davis who composed the version we are familiar with today. She called it "The Carol of the Drum." Now, her version of the song has been included as a favorite on more than one hundred popular Christmas albums.

> **...her version of the song has been included as a favorite on more than one hundred popular Christmas albums.**

The song tells the story of a young boy who wants to honor Jesus for his birthday, but the boy doesn't have a present for him. So, he decides to give him the best gift he does have. He plays a song for him on his drum. One of the stanzas talks about the little boy approaching the manger and saying that he played his best for Jesus. For that performance, the little boy gets Mary's appreciation and gratitude.

"The Little Drummer Boy" offers a great Christmas message. We can often think a gift is more valuable simply because it costs a lot of money. This song has a different message. The little boy didn't have money to offer Jesus, but he gave him something even better. The little drummer boy gave his best and honored Jesus with his song.

All of us can honor the Lord by giving our money to help people, churches, and ministries. But all of us have more to give than money. The Bible says, "For we are his workmanship, created in Christ Jesus for good works, which God prepared beforehand, that we should walk in them" (Ephesians 2:10).

All of us can honor the Lord with the example of "The Little Drummer Boy." We can give him our best by using our gifts and talents for God's good purposes.

What is the finest gift you can bring to Jesus today?

THE SONG WITH THE WRONG NUMBER

"We Three Kings"

We three kings of Orient are
Bearing gifts we traverse afar;
Field and fountain, moor and mountain,
Following yonder star.
O, star of wonder, star of light,
Star with royal beauty bright,
Westward leading, still proceeding,
Guide us to thy perfect light.

"WE THREE KINGS"

This Christmas carol is about the magi, the wise men who traveled from the East, to find the newborn King. We often think of the "Orient" as Japan or China, but the wise men were probably from the part of Asia known as Persia.

"We Three Kings" was composed in 1857 and probably has a lot more to do with our thinking than the actual passage of Scripture. The story of the magi is found in Matthew 2:1–12. Did you know that nowhere in that passage does the Bible say there were three kings?

> **...it is much more likely there would have been about twelve magi.**

In fact, it is much more likely there would have been about twelve magi. So why did this Christmas carol say there were three?

Probably because of the three gifts the Bible speaks of: gold, frankincense, and myrrh.

Why do we call these men "wise"?

The word *magi* actually meant skilled magician or astrologer. We know these men followed the star, so we believe them to be astrologers. How did these men know to follow the star?

That is a more difficult question to answer, but it's possible that, while the prophet Daniel was held captive in Babylon, he might have taught men about the promised Messiah of Israel. Daniel was considered a wise man in one of the most educated and advanced cultures of that time. Babylon was the eastern area that would be called Persia, which is known as Iran today.

The distance from Babylon to Bethlehem is 107 miles. The wise men probably lived near that region and traveled the long distance, riding camels and walking. The magi were wealthy men, and the gifts they brought were expensive. They would have brought servants to protect them, and they would have packed food, water, and tents.

When you picture the arrival of the magi, you need to think about all that the arrival meant, especially in the tiny village of Bethlehem! Jesus wasn't a baby in a manger by the time the magi arrived. The Bible uses a different word for "boy" when describing a child under the age of two. The magi might not have begun their trip until after Jesus had been born.

And one more fun fact about those "three" kings is the gifts they brought. Those valuable gifts are probably the reason Joseph, a poor man, was able to care for his family when the angel told him they all needed to flee to Egypt.

A popular saying reads: "Wise men still seek him."

Will you be wise today?

19

THE SONG INSPIRED BY LAUGHING BABIES

"Do You Hear What I Hear?"

"DO YOU HEAR WHAT I HEAR?"

"Do You Hear What I Hear?" was written in 1962 by Noël Regney, an American man.

It was a cold day in October of 1962, and Mr. Regney was walking through the streets of Manhattan. He looked at the faces of people who were scared and worried that the United States might go to war with the Russians. The Soviet Union had placed missiles in Cuba that could have been sent to almost any city in the United States. For two weeks, people were very afraid of what might happen

Noël Regney never thought he would write a Christmas carol. In fact, he said he didn't want to because Christmas had become, in his opinion, too commercial.

That night, walking through the streets of Manhattan, Mr. Regney saw two mothers taking their babies for a walk in their strollers. He found himself looking at the babies, who were smiling, laughing, and playing—and he realized he was smiling too. The babies' faces held the opposite expressions of the adults he'd seen.

So, by the time he'd arrived home, Noël Regney had composed the words to "Do You Hear What I Hear?" in his head. Later that evening, he wrote the words on paper and his wife, Gloria, wrote the music for the Christmas carol we sing today.

Sometimes, the news of our day holds stories that cause us to feel worried or afraid. The words of this Christmas carol are important to remember. Our King would want us to pray for peace—everywhere. We can remember the *holy* child of Christmas, sleeping at night, and that Jesus came to bring the world both "goodness and light."

Jesus will bring "goodness and light" this Christmas too.

Do you know how?

Jesus was talking to his disciples when he said, "You are the light of the world" (Matthew 5:14). There can be goodness and light in our world today if God's people will allow their faith to shine. That is why God gave us his Holy Spirit. We don't just "act" like a Christian. We can live as a person who has *become* like Christ, through the Holy Spirit.

A child of God is the light of the world. Will you ask Jesus to shine in your life today?

If so, he will bring light to the places you go, whenever you enter the room.

THE SONG I LOSE MY BREATH WHILE SINGING

"Angels We Have Heard on High"

Angels we have heard on high
Sweetly singing o'er the plains,
And the mountains in reply
Echoing their joyous strains.
Gloria, in excelsis Deo!

"ANGELS WE HAVE HEARD ON HIGH"

I remember feeling guilty one Sunday morning during the Christmas season. The congregation stood to sing "Angels We Have Heard on High." It is a beautiful Christmas carol, but I'm not a very talented singer.

In fact, I'm not very good at all!

So, we got to the chorus, the part where we all have to sing, "Glo-oooo-ooooo—ooooo—ooria, in excelsis Deeee— eeee-oooo!" I just pretended I was singing all those syllables. I love the words of this French Christmas carol, but I wish it had come with more "singable" music.

What does "Gloria, in excelsis Deo" mean, anyway?

I looked it up. It means "glory to God in the highest."

> It means "glory to God in the highest."

When we sing the chorus of "Angels We Have Heard on High," we are echoing the words of the angels, who proclaimed to the shepherds that their Messiah had been born. The chorus and music were written to feel like a mountain "echo" of the joyous words the angels sang.

The carol was written as an invitation for others to join with the church in a celebration of Christ during the Christmas season. One stanza says:

Come to Bethlehem and see
Him whose birth the angels sing,
Come, adore on bended knee,
Christ the Lord, the newborn King.

We often invite people to Christmas parties during this time of year. We invite people to go shopping or to see a fun movie. We invite people to join us for a lot of activities. "Angels We Have Heard on High" is a reminder that we need to invite them to worship the Christ of Christmas. He is the most important "reason for the season."

Who would come to church with you this Sunday, if you asked?

Who would enjoy singing carols with a congregation and the chance to go to your Bible class?

Who might hear and understand the real story of Christmas for the first time if you give them an invitation?

Pray about asking. Then, be brave and ask.

There are *a lot* of people in your church who are there every Sunday because *someone* invited them to come. (And tell them it's okay if they can't really sing. This preacher's wife has been getting away with it every week!)

Gloria, in excelsis Deo. Glory to God in the highest.

Jesus invites all of us to worship.

21

THE SONG ABOUT THE BOY WE SOMETIMES FORGET

"Sweet Little Jesus Boy"

"SWEET LITTLE JESUS BOY"

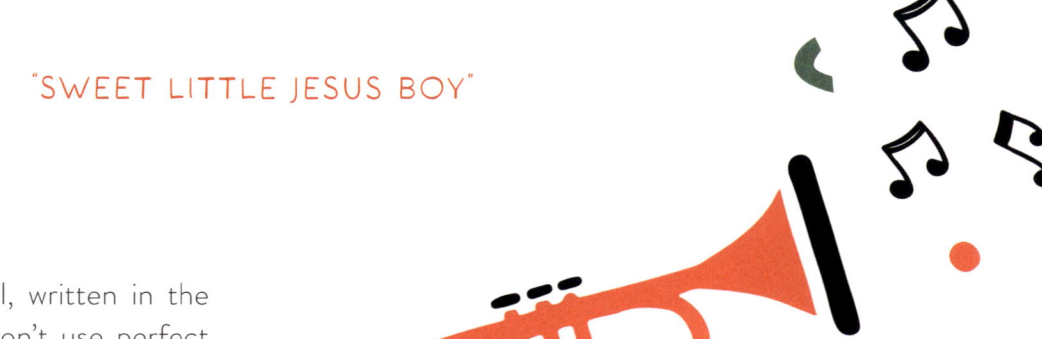

"Sweet Little Jesus Boy" is a spiritual, written in the language of an ex-slave. The words don't use perfect grammar, but they do use perfect truth.

American Robert MacGimsey was walking around New York City on Christmas Eve in 1934. He passed by one noisy bar or nightclub after another. There was a lot of loud music and a lot of Christmas celebrations, but none of the sounds he heard had *anything* to do with the true meaning of Christmas.

> **In fact, Robert MacGimsey found himself apologizing to Jesus because he realized he often left Jesus out of his celebration too.**

American slaves were often mistreated, ignored, or considered unimportant. So was Jesus. He was born in a manger because no one wanted to give up their space at the inn. The people didn't know who Jesus was.

Those people in Bethlehem didn't know that the baby born to Mary that night was the Son of God. They didn't know Jesus had been born to take all our sins away. The song says they were blind and couldn't see because they didn't know who Jesus really was.

The great depth of "Sweet Little Jesus Boy" is that the song wasn't just written about those people in Bethlehem.

It wasn't just that Jesus was mistreated by the people of his day.

The song is also about the fact that Jesus is still being mistreated by people every day.

Have you become so busy you've forgotten about Jesus today?

Have you listened to and sung songs, or celebrated and been interested in things, that have nothing to do with Jesus?

All of us have.

We still mistreat Jesus sometimes too.

But, one thing has changed.

We do *know* who Jesus was, is, and always will be.

The baby who was ignored in Bethlehem is honored and glorified today. We know who Jesus is and we know who he was.

Let's all do a better job with the way we celebrate his birthday!

THE SONG ABOUT ELECTRIFIED SHEPHERDS

"Angels From The Realms of Glory"

Angels from the realms of glory,
Wing your flight o'er all the earth;
Ye who sang creation's story
Now proclaim Messiah's birth:

Come and worship, come and worship,
Worship Christ, the newborn King.

"ANGELS FROM THE REALMS OF GLORY"

The church talks about angels more often during the Christmas season. Angels played an important role in the Christmas story. James Montgomery wanted us to sing about the Christmas angels when he wrote "Angels from the Realms of Glory."

It's impossible to imagine what it was like for the shepherds when, in the middle of the night, the sky was illuminated by the glory of the heavenly host. We live in a time when bright lights are everywhere. In fact, it is rare to ever experience complete darkness.

Shepherds lit fires at night, hoping to scare away wolves. Shepherds had the stars and the moon that gave some light during the night. But they had *never*, in all their lives, seen light like they experienced when the "angels from the realms of glory" appeared. God invented electricity a long time before Benjamin Franklin flew his kite!

> **Shepherds had the stars and the moon that gave some light during the night.**

So, what are angels doing today?

Angels are messengers and ministers from God. But what do angels look like? How do we know if we have seen one?

I've been asked a lot of questions about angels, and there is one thing I am certain of: angels exist. Jesus spoke of angels and believed in angels. We should too.

Billy Graham wrote a book called *Angels*, and it is my favorite book on the subject. Someone asked Dr. Graham if angels were real. He said, "Yes, angels are real, just as real as you and I are. Although they are largely unseen by us, they exist in great numbers. The Bible speaks of 'thousands upon 87 thousands of angels in joyful assembly' (Hebrews 12:22). When Jesus' birth was announced to the shepherds outside Bethlehem, 'a great company of the heavenly host appeared . . . praising God' (Luke 2:13)."

God created angels and uses them to serve him, speak for him, and bring him glory.

One day, I was at a stoplight, and my eyes were drawn to a man holding a cardboard sign. I always try to pray and ask God what to do. That day, I just *knew*, in my head and heart, that I was supposed to give.

When I pulled up next to him and looked him in the eyes, they were the bluest eyes I'd ever seen. He smiled and said, "God bless you."

I drove off, knowing God had *blessed*. I'm not certain I saw an angel that day, but, one day in heaven, I'm going to ask! I just know the moment was special. I still think about it today.

Hebrews 13:2 says, "Do not neglect to show hospitality to strangers, for thereby some have entertained angels unawares."

I pray God will send his angels to you this Christmas season.

THE SONG WITH A TRAGIC ORIGIN STORY

"I Heard The Bells on Christmas Day"

I heard the bells on Christmas Day
Their old, familiar carols play,
In music sweet the tones repeat
There's peace on earth, good will to men!

I thought how, as the day had come,
The belfries of all Christendom
Had rolled along th' unbroken song
Of peace on earth, good will to men!

"I HEARD THE BELLS ON CHRISTMAS DAY"

Henry Wadsworth Longfellow was an early American poet. He wrote the Christmas carol "I Heard the Bells on Christmas Day" during a particularly sad period of his life.

Longfellow's wife, Frances, had recently died from a tragic accident. She had been sealing envelopes with hot wax when a flame caught her clothes on fire. Henry had rushed to try to save her by smothering the flames and was badly burned in the process. His wife did not recover, and Longfellow was too badly burned to attend her funeral.

Two years later, the poet was once again grieved when his son, Charley, chose to enlist and fight in the Civil War—against his father's wishes. A few months later, Charley was shot, and the bullet had nicked his spine. Longfellow went to Washington to retrieve his son from the hospital. They arrived home on December 8, and Longfellow began the long process of nursing his son back to health.

Henry Wadsworth Longfellow wrote the words to "I Heard the Bells on Christmas Day" during that time. He had suffered loss and grief, but he had been greatly comforted when he heard the church bells that rang on Christmas Day. Longfellow's poem was set to music in 1872, and "I Heard the Bells" is still a song of hope and comfort to people today.

> **He had suffered loss and grief, but he had been greatly comforted when he heard the church bells that rang on Christmas Day.**

Every Christmas is a "first Christmas" for some people. It is the first Christmas after a loved one has died. It can be the first Christmas someone has to spend alone because of health problems or work responsibilities.

Do you know someone who is sad or lonely this year?

Life has lots of moments that are joyful and happy, and some that are sad. Change is part of every life. But there is a certain comfort in the things of life that do not change.

Henry Wadsworth Longfellow heard the bells ringing out that sad day, but the sounds were comforting. Those bells rang with the same music he'd heard during the happier moments of his life as well.

He was reminded of their "unbroken song" that connected him to other people in other places, and yet all of them shared the same Christmas story of "peace on earth, good will to men."

Whom do you know that needs that story of peace today?

THE SONG ABOUT LIGHT DESPITE DARK DAYS

"Joyful, Joyful We Adore Thee"

Joyful, joyful, we adore thee,
God of glory, Lord of love;
Hearts unfold like flowers before thee,
Opening to the sun above.

Melt the clouds of sin and sadness,
Drive the dark of doubt away.
Giver of immortal gladness,
Fill us with the light of day.

"JOYFUL, JOYFUL WE ADORE THEE"

Henry van Dyke had been a pastor but was a well-known professor of English literature at Princeton University when he wrote "Joyful, Joyful We Adore Thee."

Van Dyke had been visiting a friend's church when he was inspired by the beauty of the Berkshire Mountains in Williamstown, Massachusetts. He wrote the words to "Joyful, Joyful" and handed them to his friend, insisting that the words be sung to the music of Beethoven's "Ode to Joy."

This Christmas carol was written just before the beginning of World War I. People were worried about the future, but the poet wanted them to consider the Presence of God, even in the most difficult of times.

He wrote, "Melt the clouds of sin and sadness, Drive the dark of doubts away. Giver of immortal gladness, Fill us with the light of day."

Henry van Dyke knew there were reasons to be worried, but he also knew there were reasons to be joyful. Our God is a God of glory and a Lord of love.

Later in the hymn, we sing words that remind us of the character and love of Christ for all of us:

Thou art giving and forgiving,
Ever blessing, ever blest,
Wellspring of the joy of living,
Ocean depth of happy rest!
Thou our Father, Christ our Brother,
All who live in love are Thine;
Teach us how to love each other,
Lift us to the joy divine.

Jesus is the "wellspring of the joy of living." We belong to him, and he will take good care of us this Christmas. Our job is simply to love one another as Jesus has loved us.

That is how we live with the joy of Jesus, this Christmas and always.

THE SONG THAT GETS TO THE HEART OF CHRISTMAS

"O Come, O Come, Emmanuel"

O come, O come, Emmanuel,
And ransom captive Israel,
That mourns in lonely exile here
Until the Son of God appear.

Rejoice! Rejoice!
Emmanuel shall come to thee, O Israel.

"O COME, O COME, EMMANUEL"

"O Come, O Come, Emmanuel" has been sung throughout the world by God's people for more than twelve centuries. It is most often sung during the final week of Advent, as a reminder of the Magnificat, or Mary's Song, from Luke 1:46–55.

At first, the song and the melody seem to be sad and reflective of hard times. However, it's the opposite. Emmanuel is one of the names associated with Jesus. The name means "God with us."

The first verse reminds us of the many years Israel was held captive by the Babylonians and Assyrians. But the words tell those from Israel to "Rejoice! Rejoice!" Emmanuel, their promised Messiah, would come. God would be with them. On the day Christ was born in Bethlehem, Emmanuel came to dwell on the earth—and Jesus is still Emmanuel, God with us, today.

> **Emmanuel is one of the names associated with Jesus. The name means "God with us."**

The hymn has many stanzas, and each describes a hope that Christians have because of Christmas. The deepest meaning of the holiday is found in a name, Emmanuel, God with us.

The Magnificat reveals Mary's praise after realizing she had been chosen to carry and give birth to God's Son. In Luke 1:46–49, Mary sang, "My soul magnifies the Lord, and my spirit rejoices in God my Savior, for he has looked on the humble estate of his servant. For behold, from now on all generations will call me blessed; for he who is mighty has done great things for me, and holy is his name."

Mary may have been the first one to realize in amazement what it was like to have the Son of God alive and within her, but she was not to be the last. Every Christian has received God's Holy Spirit, and he is Emmanuel, God with us.

Because of Christmas, Jesus dwells within the life of every believer.

Rejoice! Rejoice! Emmanuel has come!

MERRY CHRISTMAS

AND

HAPPY NEW YEAR

We hope you enjoyed our Advent book and that it opened lots of opportunities for your family to celebrate the "joy to your world" that only Jesus brings! At Christian Parenting, we are committed to walking the parenting road alongside you as we strive to raise kids who know and love the Lord. The Advent book is just one of the many ways we hope to encourage and equip you with practical help and spiritual guidance on your parenting journey.

Parenting is an amazing privilege, but it can also be very difficult. We can draw confidence from knowing that the Lord has intentionally placed us here during this time, this day, this year, this culture, and with these kids—for a reason.

We were created for now, and God's purpose and plans are for us today! We are equipped and capable in parenting, in marriage, in ministry, and anywhere in our lives where we have given the Lord authority.

So, as you prepare for next year, we would love for you to join us at Christian Parenting as we walk the road together. Also, please check out our podcast network, where we have a podcast for every parent (and some for kids). Visit ChristianParenting.org to find out more!

Many blessings and happy new year!
The Christian Parenting Team

ABOUT JANET DENISON

Janet Denison has been writing and teaching Bible study for almost forty years and speaks with a voice that has experienced the truth of God's word. She often says the reason she gets out of bed each day is to help others understand and apply the truth of God's word to their daily lives. Teaching the Bible is her great privilege, and her goal is to help people live a life that God is able to bless.

Her ministry, Foundations with Janet Denison, exists to teach people about the transforming power of Scripture through digital Bible study and is dedicated to helping people learn how to study the Bible and apply God's truth to their lives.

Janet is a graduate of Houston Baptist University where she met her husband, Jim. They have two sons, Ryan and Craig, and four grandchildren. Janet continues to speak at church and community events in addition to her weekly local Bible study for women.

Along with her numerous Bible studies, Janet is also the author of A Great Calm, Content To Be Good, Called To Be Godly, and multiple Advent books.

ABOUT CHRISTIAN PARENTING

We want to be better parents. We want to give our children the love and attention they need. But our lives are so busy, and we're stretched so thin, it can be hard to do more than the status quo.

So we created Christian Parenting to give parents everywhere the practical and spiritual help they need, on as many platforms as possible, for free.

With the right resources given to you in the right ways, growth can happen in the midst of the busyness. You don't need to be perfect. In fact, growth comes as you embrace becoming perfectly imperfect.

Go to *ChristianParenting.org* to find out how.